Have You Seen My Vroom, Vroom?

Alisha M. Hazziez

Illustrations by
Blueberry Illustrations

Copyright © 2017 by Alisha M. Hazziez

All rights reserved.
No part of this book may be reproduced or transmitted in any form or by any means without written permission from the author.

ISBN: 978-0-692-87149-2

To my fountain of Youth:

Your love has been my foundation. I'll always encourage you to follow your passion and live the life you imagined you're never too young to start your legacy. Love, Mom.

To all my young readers: Remember you are capable of amazing things and wonderful just as you are.

It was Saturday morning. The sun was shining.

Mykel woke up, jumped out of bed, threw on his magic cape, and ran to the kitchen.

Mom was drinking coffee.
"Mom, where's my vroom, vroom?"
"Check my coat pocket."
"Okay!"

Mykel went to Mom's coat. He put his hand in the pocket.

POOF! A **half-eaten sandwich** JUMPED out! It landed on the floor with a splat.

THE SANDWICH STARTED CHASING MYKEL! MYKEL RAN INTO THE LIVING ROOM.

His dad was sleeping on the couch.

He was snoring **LOUDLY**.

Mykel **JUMPED** on dad's lap!

Dad threw his arms in the air. "Whoa, who are you running from?" Mykel smiled. "**Oooh nooobbody**. Dad, have you seen my vroom, vroom?" "No, check my computer bag?" "Ok."

Mykel ran to Dad's bag and opened it. A tablet jumped out and landed on the floor and began to chase him!

He ran into his sister Chloe's room and jumped on her bed, out of breath!

Chloe shouted, "**You little squirt, what are you doing in my room?**"

"And who are you running from, Mykel?"

"**Ooooooh nobboody**.
Chloe, have you seen my **vroom, vroom**? "No Check the pocket on my **backpack**."

Mykel replied, "Ok."

Mykel jumped off the bed. He ran to Chloe's backpack.
He unzipped the front pocket.
Pencils jumped out! Lots and lots of pencils!
"Ahhh!" yelled Mykel.

He ran into the living room.
The tablet was waiting for him. The half-eaten sandwich was waiting too!

The tablet and sandwich joined the pencils. Now they **ALL** chased Mykel!

Mykel ran into his bedroom and jumped onto his bed.

"Ouch!"

He pulled down his blanket. There was his **vroom, vroom!**

Mykel sat on his bed. The tablet, sandwich, and pencils looked up at him, shaking their tiny fists! Mykel closed his eyes **tightly** and made a wish. "I wish I were small!"

Suddenly, Mykel started to shrink!

SMALLER...AND SMALLER...

Until he was the size of his **vroom, vroom!** Mykel fixed his cape and jumped on.

He fixed his cape and **jumped** on his VROOM, VROOM.

Next, he chased the tablet back into the living room and into Dad's bag, then chased the sandwich back into the kitchen and into Mom's coat pocket.

There was Mom, still drinking her coffee. She bent down, picked Mykel up, and gave him a huge hug and kiss.
She looked at him with a warm smile.
"I see you found your **vroom, vroom.**"

Alisha Hazziez

Alisha Hazziez is a author of Have You Seen My Vroom, Vroom? and Akilah and the Red Shoes. Her fantasy series The Forgotten Codex includes The Secret Society of the Grambler Tree (co-authored) and The Chronicles of Sequestria: Journey to Triquentara.

She draws from her own life experiences to write children's books and YA novels. Her adventurous African American children's book series features her children, nieces, and nephews, who have boundless imaginations.

When she's not writing, she's testing her humor on her husband and three children, who insist her humor should stay far away from publication.

www.ingramcontent.com/pod-product-compliance
Lightning Source LLC
Chambersburg PA
CBHW081414160426
42811CB00096B/839